Lantern

poems by

Nancy Dickeman

Finishing Line Press
Georgetown, Kentucky

Lantern

For Chuck, Meris, Maia & Gabe

in memory of my mother and father

Copyright © 2018 by Nancy Dickeman
ISBN 978-1-63534-630-5 First Edition
All rights reserved under International and Pan-American Copyright Conventions.
No part of this book may be reproduced in any manner whatsoever without written permission from the publisher, except in the case of brief quotations embodied in critical articles and reviews.

ACKNOWLEDGMENTS

Grateful acknowledgment is made to the following publications in which some of these poems, sometimes in different forms or with different titles, first appeared:

The Far Field: "Nuclear Reservation"
Hawaii Pacific Review: "The Fall of 2016"
OCEAN Magazine: "Tidal Line"
Particles on the Wall: "Anniversary, Remembrance," "History's Markers, Hanford," "Blue Hills" (as "Trigger Mechanics")
Poetry Northwest: "Breathing and Dreaming"
Pontoon Poetry: "The Hallway of Burst Safeguards"
Post Road 32: "Return to Atomic City"
River City: "Comfort," "Separations" *
The Seattle Review: "Deities"
* "Separations" received a *River City* Hohenberg Award.
"The Intercessor's Grace" received a commendation in the National Poetry Competition and appeared in a *National Poetry Competition Winners Anthology*.

Publisher: Leah Maines
Editor: Christen Kincaid
Cover Art: Gabriel Williams
Author Photo: Gabriel Williams
Cover Design: Elizabeth Maines McCleavy

Printed in the USA on acid-free paper.
Order online: www.finishinglinepress.com
also available on amazon.com

Author inquiries and mail orders:
Finishing Line Press
P. O. Box 1626
Georgetown, Kentucky 40324
U. S. A.

Table of Contents

Nuclear Reservation 1
Blue Hills 2
Last Rays 3
The Intercessor's Grace 5
The Tidal Line 6
Separations 7
Deities 9
Lantern 11
Breathing and Dreaming 12
Temperance Heart 13
The Fall of 2016 14
The Girl in the Field 15
A Boy and the Trail of Debris 16
The Broken World 17
The Hallway of Burst Safeguards 18
Radioactive Tumbleweeds 19
History's Markers, Hanford 20
Anniversary, Remembrance 21
From the Edge of This World 22
Gifts 23
Sunset, A Sleight of Hand 25
Light and Harmony 26
Comfort 29
The New World 31
Return to Atomic City 33

NUCLEAR RESERVATION

Driving past security my father tipped
his hat at the guard
who waved him on. The badge
on my father's chest worn
not to name authority but
to measure exposure, the point
at which his daily risk

might trip him up. When he drove the hills
toward home the desert turned
under him, sage and sand
ground to dust, rocks overtaken by a violet glow.
All the while minerals
touched us, particulates
combing the air and marking us

invisibly changed. In the dust storm
the desert stuck to me like silt, a line
drawn around my mouth and nose.
His back to me, his face
pressed into the receiver
my father said the guards had orders:
shoot to kill. What they held

behind them was a question
of life and death:
the rods delicately working
at the purist's calculations and the tower
casting itself clean across the river, ore
reduced to powder, a golden substance
diffusible as breath.

BLUE HILLS

The blue hills rise into the blue sky.
Once their silhouette cut beyond reactors splitting
atoms, the cores lit a luminescent blue,

power spun like delicate threads, turbines
gorged with charge and plutonium cast
for the missiles readied in cornfields' silos.

Now the storage tanks' cracked hulls
leak through the earth,
the plume bound

for water, while rabbits' radioactive scat
marks the dusty ground.
Workers toil

to turn the hot waste
into glass—immutable yet destined to tick
beneath the Geiger counter's metal hand.

In the Horse Heaven Hills,
countryside once taken
for a bombing range, our dog

took to the wind,
lost beneath the uncaptured
sky. On New Year's Eve, fog slips

across the scarred hills, the Doomsday Clock
edges closer to midnight.
We watch the second hand's sweep,

lean towards heat,
the fire's spit
and raise our crackling flutes.

LAST RAYS

We lived in a wind that threw dust like flames,
carved whitecaps on the back of the Columbia.
Along the riverbank I lifted a stone
that scorched my ten-year-old palms
and tossed it back,

feeding the river, botching tips
hollered from my sisters
to make the stone skip
until my father unveiled
the world of angles, flicking the wrist
so the stone might fly hot as ash

across the rippled surface. Keeping an eye
on us all, my mother walked the silted banks
toward my father beneath the cottonwood's shadows,
his hat shielding his brow as he looked beyond
our view towards nuclear reactors rooted

along the river's curves. Back home my mother ran
the hose over the roof of our government-built house
beating down the sun's last rays
then took my hand
and walked through our K house door
its namesake plucked

from the middle of the alphabet as if striving
for balance, while plutonium
molded into discs heavier
than lead, weighted
with my father's grief and bones,
slipped quietly

into the world.
In the morning, beneath open windows
the snapdragons' velvety leaves

sagged with grit
and my mother warned
we were no match for this wind,
her brood obscured in the spinning dust
and all that harbored in the drifting clouds unseen.

THE INTERCESSOR'S GRACE

The auctioneers opened with milker units, platform scales, a gravity box
and wagon. Before lunch they had moved on
to the single seat buggy, the Speed Queen Wringer Washer that once
caught my mother's hand and by sundown

the lawn and tables were lit
with the remaining pieces: clay marbles, Depression glass
and the mahogany sleigh bed. Last came the revolvers
and military rifles, objects always kept

from sight. Somehow in the rush a few items
dropped or forgotten dotted the cut grass as if
just then set down for an outing: a red pitcher
and a torn baby coat while off to the side

in the deeper blades, a glint of wire, the sun
coiled around my grandmother's eyeglasses, the convexity
that held the world to her
as she readied the house for the returning men

out in the fields or trading
news in town: someone's boy
gone to war, carp
rustling the pond's filmy floor. Left in her bureau

was a single statue, the Virgin, blue-robed
and glowing, the gold halo signaling
virtue, the hands folded
with the intercessor's grace. By dark

there was only the must of rose water
and holy water settled
in the wood grain's curve
and bound to the articles now dispersed.

THE TIDAL LINE

Like a water bearer
I wanted to carry

the heart of the ocean
to her, settling too quickly

in her bed of sand and sleep,
my hands delivering

the sea as if even brine
might slake thirst,

salt lifted from breakers
coating the soft curve

of her brow, and the waves' rhythm
sending the tide to rush the parched shore.

It is here, in the tidal line rent
with the broken helms of whelks

and tritons, tangled kelp
holding the remnants of gulls

that she came to the waves
and to the sun blinking away

at sunset, her hands
resting and full

with life's work and worry,
the beach and the incoming sea

drumming the chambered echo
that would call her back.

SEPARATIONS

I go with my husband and child to an edge
where ocean and land meet.
We sit in the dark as if
this was the only choice,
our only hope

and we will never go back
to the house where we keep the night
beyond the windows, flushing it out
from inside with a hall lamp left burning
for daybreak. Here night begins
to open itself until we see

not its total concentration of colors,
the black, but its filtering absences,
a glow thrown from the rock beach floor
and the driftwood's heavy mass:
This sheen the underside,
the trap door through which we enter

and make ourselves at home.
Fallen asleep in her father's arms,
my daughter's face looks at four years
as it did at four months: graceful and wise.
Once I traveled so far that I could not return

within a single day. When at last I made my way above
the thinning forests and then the glaciers,
tremendous stretches of ice below me
and over the land of the Midnight Sun
returning to her, she said *I thought you were not coming*
in a voice small and unrecognizable.

The physical world depends upon
time and distance, and yet
these notions disintegrate
here on this shifting shore,
where all moments come before us
and we live in each of them, carrying ourselves
back and forth. The ocean churns
towards our driftwood fort, a rush of foam and seawater
etching a line before this vanishing, salt-crusted home.

DEITIES

> "*The mountain is the Buddha, the men are the Buddha,
> the inter-reality of all things is the Buddha and
> everything else is only a dream.*"
> —from *The Winds of Everest*, a film documenting
> the Everest ascent by the 1984 China-Everest Expedition

What they were before
was shadow. When they leave
the temple they have only
the parcels of the body and crevasses

the mind reaches.
Where they have placed themselves weather threatens
to take a life: Wind freezes
an eye, the visible
the passing light
of snow coming down
and down, earth in its new scale.
The men go higher and straight again
into the wind and then hit

clearing. In the jet stream breathing
comes hard: Near the top Chomolungma arcs
into that stream
vapor holding above her
thick as animal fur raised in wrath.
Men call her she
the way men name
earth mother or
bride. Here they fall

into her, every muscle strained
with the work of it
and they are lucky: no deaths,
one among them makes

the summit, waving at no one
and everyone. At that height forgetting
is easy, the simplest recollections
lost: who is who, which
is which, one in motion

one stationary:
a man pulling himself away
from the snow, carving
again a place for the body.

LANTERN

The hummingbird flies into red.
My father and I wager
on whether the long-necked bottle brush

or sloping petunias will draw in the beak,
hold the bird in air.
My father has come this far

to greet me, to show
the illness coloring his face.
There is nothing the far-off rolling of waves,

fishing boats cutting into port
or the farmer selling flats of berries
can do to bring us together

any more than the lantern
raised in the window,
hung by the door, will flash a signal

we might understand. Only through our hands
do we believe the means of our bodies
the way we are taken apart

and left with moonlight dimming the kerosene,
falling down through pine, through the shapes
we leave and become.

BREATHING AND DREAMING

They wake flushed with the early hour,
sleep's invitation still open, flaming like summer.
It is then we discover
them full of night's wisdom. Seamus, Anna, Dierdre,
they look to each other
recognizing temperament and sex. We stare
at their faces, the curved mouths, never
seeing ourselves, only their comprehension and whatever
might be mythical, the bed of an underground river.

Moving out and far
into rest again, we glimpse in that surrender
just before sleep something so heedless we are
alarmed. But the babies take one more
breath and go on, barely astir
in our arms; all their moments, old age and dying, blur
before us, as we rock on the hearth's brick floor,
our low wind a torch to the fire.

TEMPERANCE HEART

Facing Jim Dine's "The Blue Clamp" the paint
is layered so thick it seems there is heart
after heart, one on top of the other. Still
nothing mends the split
but a blue clamp placed at midpoint as if
pinching the two halves together. In life
what is it that holds us not coupled but
each of us singularly pointing forward
into the day? I have behind me the formica counter,
space's gray grid laid flat, the pot on the stove left
too long steaming, the child's lip
burned. If there are two people in a room
what will they each observe? The photograph snaps
the stationary objects: the carved sun dangling
from a tin-framed mirror, a blue and yellow plate
bordered with black leaves, a rounded biplane
holding the center, and then a woman crosses
the floor: who leans
towards her and who away? When the house
quiets, each room filled with a child asleep and as much
darkness as they can carry into dreams
and back again, she studies memory,
returns to the middle of conversation when one person stops
speaking and carries a question
in their eyes. What of the heart and soul,
how is it she might remember
what is not known? Take the dream, where
are the children going, shrieking
on their piggyback journey? There is matter
to organize, laundry and paperwork, a rift
that opens the ground beneath her. It is autumn, the path
covered with maple and birch leaves,
the park a hollow of reds and yellows. There is barely
time to turn the soil once more, fill it
with tulips and lilies, to enter
the earth, rich without
light and come back again.

THE FALL OF 2016

We push the baby through the crush of waterlogged leaves, past
a slumped brick wall
seared by a swastika's fresh paint.
The jagged white arms loom,
stark as hooded figures igniting
a tide of embers.

Our one-year-old grandson has his moon face,
owl face, his soft hoot-hoot, fingers clutching
a giraffe. On this walk, he points to trees
turning, their leaves wrapped
in frost, and says bus-bus-bus
slinging the s like a snake in a bed of grass.

Parting the storm waters,
the bus sends a wave over us
so that for a moment that spray,
an ocean breaker rising
from the mulch-coated city street
is all we see.

We step off the curb
hoping the ground
still lies beneath us.

THE GIRL IN THE FIELD

After a giant poster set in a Pakistani field of a girl whose parents and brother were killed in a U.S. drone strike. The poster is part of a project, "Not a Bug Splat," calling attention to civilian casualties of US drone strikes.

While the day began with a scarf
fluttering in light wind like a flag
and a child's ball kicked to the door,

by noon a drone operator
hunched at the controls in a cloaked room
saw the shapes of a young girl's parents
drifting past a fence like sails,

white dots floating across a blue screen
and unleashed the missile that fastened
onto their frames, impossible to shake loose.

On a day when the sun burst out after sudden rainfall
lighting the gold-beaded dandelions
someone knelt on the ground,
laid the orphaned girl's portrait, larger

than life, over the grass, stretching canvas the length
of a field, as if marking yardage from goalpost
to goalpost. When they stitched

the girl's image into the damp blades
her eyes faced straight into solar noon
and the drones' gray underbellies.
Now a fluff of moss covers the photo's edges,

a dandelion roots
among the splintered fibers, a stem breaking
the young girl's solemn mouth.

A BOY AND THE TRAIL OF DEBRIS

The wind's high tide swept the desert, bombs
splitting markets, homes, Baghdad, Basra.
A boy, twelve years old, plummeted
from childhood, silent as a shadow casting further
in the sand, a slip of ice melting.
Once his fingertips skimmed
a low ceiling.
Now he is the son without arms
standing among the dead: father, brother,
his mother, her stomach rounding
in the second trimester, and thirteen more
family members. He says
he will go anywhere for help
but here: the country that called him regrettable
but worth the price, and praised
the mission as cluster bombs floated
like thistledown after a bomblet
left shards in a child's skull.
Along the roadsides, depleted uranium drifts
from abandoned tanks and spent bullets,
the trail of debris cloaked in its dust.

THE BROKEN WORLD

Here, at this beginning of the broken world,
history's feuds rising,
the gray clouds at last spilled
rain across the parched dirt,
across a man with his back to the field,
where moments before, his cousins did not hold
their fire, but turned his chest
to face the sky, the rain water forking outward
over the cracked ground, the earth unable

to take in so much at once. My children
finger the globe, deciphering
the symbols: a round dark ball, a star encircled—
villages, cities, capitals, in each the markets
stocked with pears, figs, lemons, a child opening
her hands for the sweetest fruit. The seer
foretells a future much different
from expected: is this from love
taking hold in some corner,

a pinpoint on a map—
or from tragedy or disaster, something foreseen
or unforeseen devastating the planet?
I took from her vision
what I longed for most: a bouquet of flowers floating
overhead, a golden valley just out of reach
inexplicably glowing, glistening like a promise,
steps unmarked on the invisible path.

For now, a bush stands outside
the window, water heavy on each leaf,
the pane the point of intersection
between garden and house, worlds of touch
and envisioned, somewhere the soil
the color of ocher, split
into a thousand veins, and radiant.

THE HALLWAY OF BURST SAFEGUARDS

The Pacific receives
the river. Here, the plume
slips into bluer water.
It splinters

the sand. A feather floats,
a child's spoon
washes in. Upstream, sagebrush
edges riverbanks

cradling Hanford's gray halls,
birds forage
through wild grass
broken as straw.

RADIOACTIVE TUMBLEWEEDS

> *The Hanford Site, a nuclear facility on 586 square miles of land in southeastern Washington, produced the plutonium for nearly two-thirds of the US nuclear arsenal, operating from 1944-1987. It is now a large cleanup site, storing over 53 million gallons of radioactive waste. Over one million gallons of radioactive waste have leaked into the ground.*

Tumbleweeds skitter across the wild shrub steppe,
along the Columbia's grass-studded banks and past
the gray block buildings of nuclear reactors,
around the plutonium finishing plant
holding the weapons' fuel, the guard tower
with its metal cage glinting in the sun, and over
the subterranean tanks, the earth smudged
with a trail of waste.

Buffeted by gusts, the brittle plants vault
beyond the barbed-wire border,
their branches stained pink, thorns
the color of salmon
cutting beneath the river's surface,
rose-colored dye flagging
the tumbleweeds for capture.

Choked with half-lives, the skeletons
scatter through dust-riddled streets
named for the wartime generals,
past storefronts stamped
with the whirling atomic symbol,
then through yards stuffed with swing sets
and birch trees. They careen past fence-lines
and through downwind farms
strung on a map with signposts:
a chamber of Xs for the damaged hearts,
a constellation of Os for cancers.

Elusive, the tumbleweeds spin
over the broken earth.

HISTORY'S MARKERS, HANFORD

Wind sweeps sand across basins,
swirling it through tank farms
stocked with sludge.

In the upturned earth, history's markers
seep like tracers through
the hard beds of rock and soil,
a faint pulse
that sets the Geiger counter clicking.

Here, secrecy and science forged
against the push of sand

and wind, workers bent to their task,
grit in their mouths, a film of dust gracing
their cheekbones, entering the nose

the eyelids' border, while plutonium
yielded for Fat Man's core.
And there, Bockscar opened its hatches
over Nagasaki, birds in flight

burst into flame, women and children
turned to shadow in stone.

Hear the desert tick
the herons' ragged course
veering across the river
elements dispersed through silt
a burial's feathered trajectory.

ANNIVERSARY, REMEMBRANCE

After a summer of calm and heat
the pink calla lily's one bloom
curled under, the day has fallen
to wind and water, the lake's still sheen
overcome with concentric crests. A crowd
has gathered in remembrance, Hiroshima
and Nagasaki caught beneath their tongues
fusion of history and the unspeakable
moment when light shattered
the city, a man pushing a cart turned

to shadow, a figure wrapped around a huge cup
as though the skeleton
were indelible, the image burnished
into the stone path. There is no
absolution, only sorrow, lanterns set in the water
with hope the dead may rest. The crowd lines
the dock lowering the lit boxes
into the lake, the ramp glowing with candlelight
and the bent shapes. I have sent mine off
with shared wishes for the past and future,

time's culmination. The thick stalks along the bank
weave a line that holds
the lanterns returned to shore,
paper sheaths singed by flame,
smoke and ash floating
across the moon's changing face in the water—
shard, flask, a scrim of filament
and fossil—and across the open wild irises,
their yellow petals flared
like torches circling the lake.

FROM THE EDGE OF THIS WORLD

On a night saddled with unfinished sentences,
story problems with their remnants of apples

spread across the worn kitchen table,
children colored the stone steps

beneath the half-moon and the street lamp's errant
light, abandoned their drawings for a chance to be spun

above the yard of grass and juniper.
With the boy hooked in the father's arms, the pair flew

from the uneven slope
over rock and shrub, leaving

the flat surface of the earth
and lifting towards the Big Dipper

and the scattershot trail of comet dust.
Rejecting the willowy stars

the two dropped,
descending to search for the earth's rich matter:

soil, feather, bone,
crawling in the realm

belonging to animals
and the past. Then they rose from all fours

brushed off the dirt and pine needles
and walked through the center of night

into the open house, a single light flickering,
a wooden cave aglow.

GIFTS

The magnolia
drops its brown pods,
soft and split
like a heart, the webbed parting

of fingers, the tree carrying
its huge flowers in the shape of flames
or a host of chalices:
the petals curled like a rim

forged
so the wine will fall
into the parted mouth.
From a scrap of grass, I scan

the evening sky for a comet moving faster
than my eye, place it
west of the Big Dipper—a smear,
a blurred orb darting

from the binoculars' field of vision,
this our glimpse
into time, through calamity and longing:
the cat caught beneath the moving car,

the train's crossbar lowering
down to the rooftop,
clouds taking shape and rising.
The hawthorn faces the North Star,

its branches arced like the body's palm,
sheaths of leaf and thorn pushing upward
as if bearing gifts.
The world shifts,

about to slip open
and I am ready
to drink, to lift the water
from the stream bed,

to stand under the comet's path
and finish this thirst.

A SUNSET, A SLEIGHT OF HAND

I imagined the sun falling
last night in Sweden
like a million crushed suns,

shards of light clustered over Gothenburg,
the rooftops' clay tiles, the sky
turning the blush of plums'
flesh and skin, lasts light's colors

spilling into a sunset like the one
we saw travelling there years ago
when our daughter called for us
from the other side of the spinning globe

and once back we waited together
for her siblings to arrive
which they would soon do,
born in two quick bursts.

Today, rainfall brought down the earth
while fires to the south claimed lives,
houses and wine country. From the opposite coast
the president took the podium like a magician

with a flash of red fluttering,
trying to persuade us
to lay our hands on flames
even as the flaring tips surround us.

LIGHT AND HARMONY

1. *Death*

Here it is, the family thinks,
gathering around the sickbed.
The mother, the ill man's wife, grieves
at her forthcoming loss. He wants
his coat, his clothes hung up,
wants to know how all this—his life's tragic events—
occurred. It is spring. Children
flood the outdoors and soon we will see the bridge

the hopeless must cross
to summer and the moon
in its amber transformations. When this man,
my father, slips further
into the coma the nurses say
He is sleeping heavily and won't know you

are there. Scientists say the hearing
is the last of the senses to go.
I depended upon
touch, silent thought. They draw
the white curtain
around the small configuration
of my father's room and it is a deathbed
we hover about. I know the stories
about the soul rising

above the body and the invasion of light,
the spirit's blank hue. At the burial
the sun breaks the day
and all the friends he longed
to see give us the anecdotes of his life.
When the sun comes out it is an omen
the dead one lived

a good life. So this we take—hungry shoppers
at the market—whatever good word and idea do
for the heart. Now the house is a conservatory bursting
with exotic blossoms, death the land
even the living
explore, the land that thrives within us.

2. *The Children*

The children do not behave
the way the adults expect. They are in love
with things that grow:
field tulip, star of Bethlehem,
the pumpkin blossom with its yellow flutes
and the plum, those hanging
on the low wet limbs, the splitting
ground fall. Each night, they explain, we all dream:
Theirs is the dream of the snowy room.

My dream is filled with a green cave
stung with stalactites
a dripping salt cavern.
When parents scold for their lives' frustrations
the children cover their ears, a conch
calling them out to sea. In their watercolors
they will have nothing

of the happy face. They paint
anger and purity, rainbows
hung on a red lattice.

Beyond this we swim
or play, the wooden trains stall on the track.
Does the sewn cat move at night?

Riddles and rhymes
are what we live by.
We run from fence
to fence in a choreographed dance, a jig
for the imaginary film. Tomorrow they will want
to play with the screen and keys
creating a green turtle surrounded
by green lines, trapped
in a box.

3. *Work*

This is the business of our lives,
the constant bartering
for the future. In an office I looked out
on water, birds scavenging
against the huge backdrop. There I did the tasks
that keep things going as they do.
When I first reached
my father's spirit
he was still angry at his life's turning

spelling out the letters s-o-b, a curse
or lament. The runes counsel
Live the ordinary life in a non-ordinary way
and I try to discover
how to live in a world
filled with the extraordinary
and history's horrific events. I listen
as the tin whistle cuts
across scales, grief and joy
lit through the chambers of our imperfect hearts.

COMFORT

> *"Sometimes what's wrong does not hurt at all, but rather shines like a new moon."*   —Mary Oliver

In morning light sun hits the scarred table
and in the kitchen tea water

hisses: the hiss and steam of labor.
In the time it takes the pot to boil

light edges further
onto the table, a cat hunches

waiting for prey and the crow flies straight
into the core of electrical connections.

There is the labor of tasks (a plenitude
of gathering and arranging to occupy

a lifetime) and the strain of work that bends
a life: the bone's crack grown louder until

it either splinters irreversibly
or begins the series of shifts

and mends. What occurs after labor may not
be what was expected but gives

no reason for surprise. My husband
speaks of comfort, my child

of death. The three of us sit on a bench
watching tomatoes bend their bulky green plants

back down to ground. I am wrong
to think the child's griefs are bound

only to the known, the physical parameters.
She has still her face of fire

and fears. The human world bears
its accumulation of evidence: a world

split like an apple cut for the star,
a cartography of boundaries and across

it all the hired hands setting about their work.
In the clear sky the evening star is a smudge

and the constellations are full
with suns collapsing: an involution, as if

the universe were shrinking or assuming
new form behind the black holes:

either of shrinkage or expansion, the processes
equally violent, a path

studded with disturbances, gleaming.

THE NEW WORLD

Philosophers set their theories afloat
watching time swing like a circle around
the tomato sliced with the evening meal.
In another room, poring through

the heavy texts, mathematicians make calculations.
Rain falls down, first rising
over the leaf-studded drains, then
spilling like a mutable solid onto the vanishing

ground. A musician holds the notes in air
and on a day when her lungs are full
lets out a trill in the last note's
final moment. There is the split

second that eludes detection before the world
shifts: before the earth's plates
slip and the ground first rolls, then lurches
and children fold themselves

beneath school desks, parents at work list
like ships while the giant buildings
shimmy and an earthquake's force
wobbles the earth on its axis

changing time. Driving for hours
forests of pine and cedar give way
to the long fetch of desert, the moon slung
like a cast in the violet sky

announcing in its shrouded light
the new world, rifts
centered in time and geology,
my mother singing her way

into the garden's glistening roots,
past first light, past late snow capping
the dormant lavender and there, an entrance,
space's newly made curvature.

RETURN TO ATOMIC CITY

One day I return, standing
at the house where my father hunched
over the periodic table and my mother
scrubbed the sandstorm's grit
from my face.

The tour bus drives through Hanford's acres, past
the cocooned cores, past the B Reactor
in whose tall rooms plutonium was rushed
for the second bomb, falling
so quickly on the heels
of the first dead.

The bus heaves
past the sacred rolling mounds
the tribes call Mooli Mooli,
pausing at the subterranean
storage tanks. Here radioactive waste crosses
the boundaries of its metal shells,
slipping into the earth.

Nightfall, and the moon flares
like a spindle of fire on the river.
I plunge my hands beneath the surface
but nothing washes off,
the hot particulates long ago
burrowed into me.

ADDITIONAL ACKNOWLEDGMENTS

A wellspring of gratitude goes to poets across geographies and time who helped make these poems and this book possible, especially Suzanne Matson, for wisdom and guidance, always; JM Miller for insights and suggestions with the poems and their gathering; Sharon Bryan, a keen eye, then and now. An immense thank-you also goes out to Kathleen Flenniken, Steven Goldsberry, Valerie Martinez and Scott T. Starbuck. Thank you Kim Cope Tait, Sylvia Rains Dennis, Toby Goostree. Applause to Dottie Ashley, turning poetry to song.

Thank you to those at Finishing Line Press, especially Leah Maines and Christen Kincaid.

For the luminous cover art, "Lightsource," deepest thanks to Gabriel Williams.

A warm embrace and much love to: my home crew, Chuck, who read and re-read, my children Meris, Maia and Gabe, who each cast bright lights, along with their spouses, Mark, Joy and Nicole, plus those spritely sparks, Ronan and Graham; the Dickeman, Guillen, Wright broods, especially daughters of dust Mary, Dianne, Marcia and Kathy (with a tip of the hat to Kathy for her editing eye) and dear friends and helpers, near and far.

Nancy Dickeman's poems, fiction and essays appear in *Post Road, Poetry Northwest, The Seattle Review, Hawaii Pacific Review, Pontoon Poetry, River City, The Seattle PI, OCEAN Magazine, Common Dreams* and other publications. She received her MA in Creative Writing at the University of Washington where she won an Academy of American Poets Award. She has recently completed a full-length poetry collection, *Our Crackling Flutes*, and two novel manuscripts, *The Wind-Scattered World*, a nuclear age story, and a middle grade fantasy, *The Diving Girl and the Sunken Forest*.

While she currently lives in Seattle, Nancy grew up in the atomic town of Richland, Washington, the bedroom community for the Hanford Site, where the plutonium for the Fat Man bomb dropped on Nagasaki was produced, and now known as the most contaminated site in the western hemisphere. Nancy is co-founder and literary curator for a multidisciplinary exhibit addressing nuclear issues, *Particles on the Wall*.

Lantern is her debut poetry collection. www.nancydickeman.com.

www.ingramcontent.com/pod-product-compliance
Lightning Source LLC
LaVergne TN
LVHW041602070426
835507LV00011B/1250